# SCRIPTURE
# JOURNAL

ENGLISH STANDARD VERSION

## 1–2 TIMOTHY
## &
## TITUS

CROSSW

WHEATON, ILLINOIS

ESV® Scripture Journal: 1–2 Timothy and Titus

The Holy Bible, English Standard Version® (ESV®)
Copyright © 2001 by Crossway,
a publishing ministry of Good News Publishers.
All rights reserved.

ESV® Text Edition: 2016

Printed in China
Published by Crossway
Wheaton, Illinois 60187, U.S.A.
crossway.org

Crossway is a not-for-profit publishing ministry that exists solely for the purpose of publishing the Good News of the Gospel and the Truth of God's Word, the Bible. A portion of the purchase price of every ESV Bible is donated to help support Bible distribution ministry around the world.

The ESV Bible is free online and on mobile devices everywhere worldwide, including a selection of free Bible resources, at esv.org.

| RRDS | 30 | 29 | 28 | 27 | 26 | 25 | 24 | 23 |
|------|----|----|----|----|----|----|----|----|
| 19 | 18 | 17 | 16 | 15 | 14 | 13 | 12 | 11 | 10 |

# PREFACE

## The Bible

The words of the Bible are the very words of God our Creator speaking to us. They are completely truthful;[1] they are pure;[2] they are powerful;[3] and they are wise and righteous.[4] We should read these words with reverence and awe,[5] and with joy and delight.[6] Through these words God gives us eternal life,[7] and daily nourishes our spiritual lives.[8]

## The ESV Translation

The English Standard Version® (ESV®) stands in the classic stream of English Bible translations that goes back nearly five centuries. In this stream, accurate faithfulness to the original text is combined with simplicity, beauty, and dignity of expression. Our goal has been to carry forward this legacy for this generation and generations to come.

The ESV is an "essentially literal" translation that seeks as far as possible to reproduce the meaning and structure of the original text and the personal style of each Bible writer. We have sought to be "as literal as possible" while maintaining clear expression and literary excellence. Therefore the ESV is well suited for both personal reading and church ministry, for devotional reflection and serious study, and for Scripture memorization.

---

[1] Ps. 119:160; Prov. 30:5; Titus 1:2; Heb. 6:18  [2] Ps. 12:6  [3] Jer. 23:29; Heb. 4:12; 1 Pet. 1:23
[4] Ps. 19:7–11  [5] Deut. 28:58; Ps. 119:74; Isa. 66:2  [6] Ps. 19:7–11; 119:14, 97, 103; Jer. 15:16
[7] John 6:68; 1 Pet. 1:23  [8] Deut. 32:46; Matt. 4:4

## The ESV Publishing Team

The ESV publishing team has included more than a hundred people. The fourteen-member Translation Oversight Committee benefited from the work of fifty biblical experts serving as Translation Review Scholars and from the comments of the more than fifty members of the Advisory Council. This international team from many denominations shares a common commitment to the truth of God's Word and to historic Christian orthodoxy.

## To God's Honor and Praise

We know that no Bible translation is perfect; but we also know that God uses imperfect and inadequate things to his honor and praise. So to God the Father, Son, and Holy Spirit— and to his people—we offer what we have done, with our prayers that it may prove useful, with gratitude for much help given, and with ongoing wonder that our God should ever have entrusted to us so momentous a task.

To God alone be the glory!
The Translation Oversight Committee

# 1 TIMOTHY

## Greeting

**1** Paul, an apostle of Christ Jesus by command of God our Savior and of Christ Jesus our hope, ² To Timothy, my true child in the faith:

Grace, mercy, and peace from God the Father and Christ Jesus our Lord.

## Warning Against False Teachers

³ As I urged you when I was going to Macedonia, remain at Ephesus so that you may charge certain persons not to teach any different doctrine, ⁴ nor to devote themselves to myths and endless genealogies, which promote speculations rather than the stewardship from God that is by faith. ⁵ The aim of our charge is love that issues from a pure heart and a good conscience and a sincere faith. ⁶ Certain persons, by swerving from these, have wandered away into vain discussion, ⁷ desiring to be teachers of the law, without understanding either what they are saying or the things about which they make confident assertions.

⁸ Now we know that the law is good, if one uses it lawfully, ⁹ understanding this, that the law is not laid down for the just but for the lawless and disobedient, for the ungodly and sinners, for the unholy and profane, for those who strike their fathers and mothers, for murderers, ¹⁰ the sexually immoral,

men who practice homosexuality, enslavers, liars, perjurers, and whatever else is contrary to sound doctrine, [11] in accordance with the gospel of the glory of the blessed God with which I have been entrusted.

### Christ Jesus Came to Save Sinners

[12] I thank him who has given me strength, Christ Jesus our Lord, because he judged me faithful, appointing me to his service, [13] though formerly I was a blasphemer, persecutor, and insolent opponent. But I received mercy because I had acted ignorantly in unbelief, [14] and the grace of our Lord overflowed for me with the faith and love that are in Christ Jesus. [15] The saying is trustworthy and deserving of full acceptance, that Christ Jesus came into the world to save sinners, of whom I am the foremost. [16] But I received mercy for this reason, that in me, as the foremost, Jesus Christ might display his perfect patience as an example to those who were to believe in him for eternal life. [17] To the King of the ages, immortal, invisible, the only God, be honor and glory forever and ever. Amen.

[18] This charge I entrust to you, Timothy, my child, in accordance with the prophecies previously made about you, that by them you may wage the good warfare, [19] holding faith and a good conscience. By rejecting this, some have made shipwreck of their faith, [20] among whom are Hymenaeus and Alexander, whom I have handed over to Satan that they may learn not to blaspheme.

### Pray for All People

2 First of all, then, I urge that supplications, prayers, intercessions, and thanksgivings be made for all people, [2] for kings and all who are in high positions, that we may lead a

peaceful and quiet life, godly and dignified in every way. ³This is good, and it is pleasing in the sight of God our Savior, ⁴who desires all people to be saved and to come to the knowledge of the truth. ⁵For there is one God, and there is one mediator between God and men, the man Christ Jesus, ⁶who gave himself as a ransom for all, which is the testimony given at the proper time. ⁷For this I was appointed a preacher and an apostle (I am telling the truth, I am not lying), a teacher of the Gentiles in faith and truth.

⁸I desire then that in every place the men should pray, lifting holy hands without anger or quarreling; ⁹likewise also that women should adorn themselves in respectable apparel, with modesty and self-control, not with braided hair and gold or pearls or costly attire, ¹⁰but with what is proper for women who profess godliness—with good works. ¹¹Let a woman learn quietly with all submissiveness. ¹²I do not permit a woman to teach or to exercise authority over a man; rather, she is to remain quiet. ¹³For Adam was formed first, then Eve; ¹⁴and Adam was not deceived, but the woman was deceived and became a transgressor. ¹⁵Yet she will be saved through childbearing—if they continue in faith and love and holiness, with self-control.

### Qualifications for Overseers

**3** The saying is trustworthy: If anyone aspires to the office of overseer, he desires a noble task. ²Therefore an overseer must be above reproach, the husband of one wife, soberminded, self-controlled, respectable, hospitable, able to teach, ³not a drunkard, not violent but gentle, not quarrelsome, not a lover of money. ⁴He must manage his own household well, with all dignity keeping his children submissive, ⁵for if

someone does not know how to manage his own household, how will he care for God's church? [6] He must not be a recent convert, or he may become puffed up with conceit and fall into the condemnation of the devil. [7] Moreover, he must be well thought of by outsiders, so that he may not fall into disgrace, into a snare of the devil.

### Qualifications for Deacons

[8] Deacons likewise must be dignified, not double-tongued, not addicted to much wine, not greedy for dishonest gain. [9] They must hold the mystery of the faith with a clear conscience. [10] And let them also be tested first; then let them serve as deacons if they prove themselves blameless. [11] Their wives likewise must be dignified, not slanderers, but sober-minded, faithful in all things. [12] Let deacons each be the husband of one wife, managing their children and their own households well. [13] For those who serve well as deacons gain a good standing for themselves and also great confidence in the faith that is in Christ Jesus.

### The Mystery of Godliness

[14] I hope to come to you soon, but I am writing these things to you so that, [15] if I delay, you may know how one ought to behave in the household of God, which is the church of the living God, a pillar and buttress of the truth. [16] Great indeed, we confess, is the mystery of godliness:

> He was manifested in the flesh,
>     vindicated by the Spirit,
>         seen by angels,

> proclaimed among the nations,
> believed on in the world,
> taken up in glory.

## Some Will Depart from the Faith

**4** Now the Spirit expressly says that in later times some will depart from the faith by devoting themselves to deceitful spirits and teachings of demons, ² through the insincerity of liars whose consciences are seared, ³ who forbid marriage and require abstinence from foods that God created to be received with thanksgiving by those who believe and know the truth. ⁴ For everything created by God is good, and nothing is to be rejected if it is received with thanksgiving, ⁵ for it is made holy by the word of God and prayer.

## A Good Servant of Christ Jesus

⁶ If you put these things before the brothers, you will be a good servant of Christ Jesus, being trained in the words of the faith and of the good doctrine that you have followed. ⁷ Have nothing to do with irreverent, silly myths. Rather train yourself for godliness; ⁸ for while bodily training is of some value, godliness is of value in every way, as it holds promise for the present life and also for the life to come. ⁹ The saying is trustworthy and deserving of full acceptance. ¹⁰ For to this end we toil and strive, because we have our hope set on the living God, who is the Savior of all people, especially of those who believe.

¹¹ Command and teach these things. ¹² Let no one despise you for your youth, but set the believers an example in speech, in conduct, in love, in faith, in purity. ¹³ Until I come, devote yourself to the public reading of Scripture, to exhortation, to

teaching. [14] Do not neglect the gift you have, which was given you by prophecy when the council of elders laid their hands on you. [15] Practice these things, immerse yourself in them, so that all may see your progress. [16] Keep a close watch on yourself and on the teaching. Persist in this, for by so doing you will save both yourself and your hearers.

*Instructions for the Church*

5 Do not rebuke an older man but encourage him as you would a father, younger men as brothers, [2] older women as mothers, younger women as sisters, in all purity.

[3] Honor widows who are truly widows. [4] But if a widow has children or grandchildren, let them first learn to show godliness to their own household and to make some return to their parents, for this is pleasing in the sight of God. [5] She who is truly a widow, left all alone, has set her hope on God and continues in supplications and prayers night and day, [6] but she who is self-indulgent is dead even while she lives. [7] Command these things as well, so that they may be without reproach. [8] But if anyone does not provide for his relatives, and especially for members of his household, he has denied the faith and is worse than an unbeliever.

[9] Let a widow be enrolled if she is not less than sixty years of age, having been the wife of one husband, [10] and having a reputation for good works: if she has brought up children, has shown hospitality, has washed the feet of the saints, has cared for the afflicted, and has devoted herself to every good work. [11] But refuse to enroll younger widows, for when their passions draw them away from Christ, they desire to marry [12] and so incur condemnation for having abandoned their former faith.

¹³ Besides that, they learn to be idlers, going about from house to house, and not only idlers, but also gossips and busybodies, saying what they should not. ¹⁴ So I would have younger widows marry, bear children, manage their households, and give the adversary no occasion for slander. ¹⁵ For some have already strayed after Satan. ¹⁶ If any believing woman has relatives who are widows, let her care for them. Let the church not be burdened, so that it may care for those who are truly widows.

¹⁷ Let the elders who rule well be considered worthy of double honor, especially those who labor in preaching and teaching. ¹⁸ For the Scripture says, "You shall not muzzle an ox when it treads out the grain," and, "The laborer deserves his wages." ¹⁹ Do not admit a charge against an elder except on the evidence of two or three witnesses. ²⁰ As for those who persist in sin, rebuke them in the presence of all, so that the rest may stand in fear. ²¹ In the presence of God and of Christ Jesus and of the elect angels I charge you to keep these rules without prejudging, doing nothing from partiality. ²² Do not be hasty in the laying on of hands, nor take part in the sins of others; keep yourself pure. ²³ (No longer drink only water, but use a little wine for the sake of your stomach and your frequent ailments.) ²⁴ The sins of some people are conspicuous, going before them to judgment, but the sins of others appear later. ²⁵ So also good works are conspicuous, and even those that are not cannot remain hidden.

6 Let all who are under a yoke as bondservants regard their own masters as worthy of all honor, so that the name of God and the teaching may not be reviled. ² Those who have believing masters must not be disrespectful on the ground that they are brothers; rather they must serve all the better

since those who benefit by their good service are believers and beloved.

### False Teachers and True Contentment

Teach and urge these things. ³ If anyone teaches a different doctrine and does not agree with the sound words of our Lord Jesus Christ and the teaching that accords with godliness, ⁴ he is puffed up with conceit and understands nothing. He has an unhealthy craving for controversy and for quarrels about words, which produce envy, dissension, slander, evil suspicions, ⁵ and constant friction among people who are depraved in mind and deprived of the truth, imagining that godliness is a means of gain. ⁶ But godliness with contentment is great gain, ⁷ for we brought nothing into the world, and we cannot take anything out of the world. ⁸ But if we have food and clothing, with these we will be content. ⁹ But those who desire to be rich fall into temptation, into a snare, into many senseless and harmful desires that plunge people into ruin and destruction. ¹⁰ For the love of money is a root of all kinds of evils. It is through this craving that some have wandered away from the faith and pierced themselves with many pangs.

### Fight the Good Fight of Faith

¹¹ But as for you, O man of God, flee these things. Pursue righteousness, godliness, faith, love, steadfastness, gentleness. ¹² Fight the good fight of the faith. Take hold of the eternal life to which you were called and about which you made the good confession in the presence of many witnesses. ¹³ I charge you in the presence of God, who gives life to all things, and of Christ Jesus, who in his testimony before Pontius Pilate made the

good confession, [14] to keep the commandment unstained and free from reproach until the appearing of our Lord Jesus Christ, [15] which he will display at the proper time—he who is the blessed and only Sovereign, the King of kings and Lord of lords, [16] who alone has immortality, who dwells in unapproachable light, whom no one has ever seen or can see. To him be honor and eternal dominion. Amen.

[17] As for the rich in this present age, charge them not to be haughty, nor to set their hopes on the uncertainty of riches, but on God, who richly provides us with everything to enjoy. [18] They are to do good, to be rich in good works, to be generous and ready to share, [19] thus storing up treasure for themselves as a good foundation for the future, so that they may take hold of that which is truly life.

[20] O Timothy, guard the deposit entrusted to you. Avoid the irreverent babble and contradictions of what is falsely called "knowledge," [21] for by professing it some have swerved from the faith.

Grace be with you.

# 2 TIMOTHY

## Greeting

1 Paul, an apostle of Christ Jesus by the will of God according to the promise of the life that is in Christ Jesus,

² To Timothy, my beloved child:

Grace, mercy, and peace from God the Father and Christ Jesus our Lord.

## Guard the Deposit Entrusted to You

³ I thank God whom I serve, as did my ancestors, with a clear conscience, as I remember you constantly in my prayers night and day. ⁴ As I remember your tears, I long to see you, that I may be filled with joy. ⁵ I am reminded of your sincere faith, a faith that dwelt first in your grandmother Lois and your mother Eunice and now, I am sure, dwells in you as well. ⁶ For this reason I remind you to fan into flame the gift of God, which is in you through the laying on of my hands, ⁷ for God gave us a spirit not of fear but of power and love and self-control.

⁸ Therefore do not be ashamed of the testimony about our Lord, nor of me his prisoner, but share in suffering for the gospel by the power of God, ⁹ who saved us and called us to a holy calling, not because of our works but because of his own purpose and grace, which he gave us in Christ Jesus before the ages began, ¹⁰ and which now has been manifested through

the appearing of our Savior Christ Jesus, who abolished death and brought life and immortality to light through the gospel, [11] for which I was appointed a preacher and apostle and teacher, [12] which is why I suffer as I do. But I am not ashamed, for I know whom I have believed, and I am convinced that he is able to guard until that day what has been entrusted to me. [13] Follow the pattern of the sound words that you have heard from me, in the faith and love that are in Christ Jesus. [14] By the Holy Spirit who dwells within us, guard the good deposit entrusted to you.

[15] You are aware that all who are in Asia turned away from me, among whom are Phygelus and Hermogenes. [16] May the Lord grant mercy to the household of Onesiphorus, for he often refreshed me and was not ashamed of my chains, [17] but when he arrived in Rome he searched for me earnestly and found me— [18] may the Lord grant him to find mercy from the Lord on that day!—and you well know all the service he rendered at Ephesus.

### A Good Soldier of Christ Jesus

2 You then, my child, be strengthened by the grace that is in Christ Jesus, [2] and what you have heard from me in the presence of many witnesses entrust to faithful men, who will be able to teach others also. [3] Share in suffering as a good soldier of Christ Jesus. [4] No soldier gets entangled in civilian pursuits, since his aim is to please the one who enlisted him. [5] An athlete is not crowned unless he competes according to the rules. [6] It is the hard-working farmer who ought to have the first share of the crops. [7] Think over what I say, for the Lord will give you understanding in everything.

⁸ Remember Jesus Christ, risen from the dead, the offspring of David, as preached in my gospel, ⁹ for which I am suffering, bound with chains as a criminal. But the word of God is not bound! ¹⁰ Therefore I endure everything for the sake of the elect, that they also may obtain the salvation that is in Christ Jesus with eternal glory. ¹¹ The saying is trustworthy, for:

> If we have died with him, we will also live with him;
>
> ¹² if we endure, we will also reign with him;
>
> if we deny him, he also will deny us;
>
> ¹³ if we are faithless, he remains faithful—

for he cannot deny himself.

### A Worker Approved by God

¹⁴ Remind them of these things, and charge them before God not to quarrel about words, which does no good, but only ruins the hearers. ¹⁵ Do your best to present yourself to God as one approved, a worker who has no need to be ashamed, rightly handling the word of truth. ¹⁶ But avoid irreverent babble, for it will lead people into more and more ungodliness, ¹⁷ and their talk will spread like gangrene. Among them are Hymenaeus and Philetus, ¹⁸ who have swerved from the truth, saying that the resurrection has already happened. They are upsetting the faith of some. ¹⁹ But God's firm foundation stands, bearing this seal: "The Lord knows those who are his," and, "Let everyone who names the name of the Lord depart from iniquity."

²⁰ Now in a great house there are not only vessels of gold and silver but also of wood and clay, some for honorable use, some for dishonorable. ²¹ Therefore, if anyone cleanses himself from

what is dishonorable, he will be a vessel for honorable use, set apart as holy, useful to the master of the house, ready for every good work.

²² So flee youthful passions and pursue righteousness, faith, love, and peace, along with those who call on the Lord from a pure heart. ²³ Have nothing to do with foolish, ignorant controversies; you know that they breed quarrels. ²⁴ And the Lord's servant must not be quarrelsome but kind to everyone, able to teach, patiently enduring evil, ²⁵ correcting his opponents with gentleness. God may perhaps grant them repentance leading to a knowledge of the truth, ²⁶ and they may come to their senses and escape from the snare of the devil, after being captured by him to do his will.

*Godlessness in the Last Days*

3 But understand this, that in the last days there will come times of difficulty. ² For people will be lovers of self, lovers of money, proud, arrogant, abusive, disobedient to their parents, ungrateful, unholy, ³ heartless, unappeasable, slanderous, without self-control, brutal, not loving good, ⁴ treacherous, reckless, swollen with conceit, lovers of pleasure rather than lovers of God, ⁵ having the appearance of godliness, but denying its power. Avoid such people. ⁶ For among them are those who creep into households and capture weak women, burdened with sins and led astray by various passions, ⁷ always learning and never able to arrive at a knowledge of the truth. ⁸ Just as Jannes and Jambres opposed Moses, so these men also oppose the truth, men corrupted in mind and disqualified regarding the faith. ⁹ But they will not get very far, for their folly will be plain to all, as was that of those two men.

*All Scripture Is Breathed Out by God*

**¹⁰** You, however, have followed my teaching, my conduct, my aim in life, my faith, my patience, my love, my steadfastness, **¹¹** my persecutions and sufferings that happened to me at Antioch, at Iconium, and at Lystra—which persecutions I endured; yet from them all the Lord rescued me. **¹²** Indeed, all who desire to live a godly life in Christ Jesus will be persecuted, **¹³** while evil people and impostors will go on from bad to worse, deceiving and being deceived. **¹⁴** But as for you, continue in what you have learned and have firmly believed, knowing from whom you learned it **¹⁵** and how from childhood you have been acquainted with the sacred writings, which are able to make you wise for salvation through faith in Christ Jesus. **¹⁶** All Scripture is breathed out by God and profitable for teaching, for reproof, for correction, and for training in righteousness, **¹⁷** that the man of God may be complete, equipped for every good work.

*Preach the Word*

**4** I charge you in the presence of God and of Christ Jesus, who is to judge the living and the dead, and by his appearing and his kingdom: **²** preach the word; be ready in season and out of season; reprove, rebuke, and exhort, with complete patience and teaching. **³** For the time is coming when people will not endure sound teaching, but having itching ears they will accumulate for themselves teachers to suit their own passions, **⁴** and will turn away from listening to the truth and wander off into myths. **⁵** As for you, always be sober-minded, endure suffering, do the work of an evangelist, fulfill your ministry.

**⁶** For I am already being poured out as a drink offering, and the time of my departure has come. **⁷** I have fought the good

fight, I have finished the race, I have kept the faith. [8] Henceforth there is laid up for me the crown of righteousness, which the Lord, the righteous judge, will award to me on that day, and not only to me but also to all who have loved his appearing.

### Personal Instructions

[9] Do your best to come to me soon. [10] For Demas, in love with this present world, has deserted me and gone to Thessalonica. Crescens has gone to Galatia, Titus to Dalmatia. [11] Luke alone is with me. Get Mark and bring him with you, for he is very useful to me for ministry. [12] Tychicus I have sent to Ephesus. [13] When you come, bring the cloak that I left with Carpus at Troas, also the books, and above all the parchments. [14] Alexander the coppersmith did me great harm; the Lord will repay him according to his deeds. [15] Beware of him yourself, for he strongly opposed our message. [16] At my first defense no one came to stand by me, but all deserted me. May it not be charged against them! [17] But the Lord stood by me and strengthened me, so that through me the message might be fully proclaimed and all the Gentiles might hear it. So I was rescued from the lion's mouth. [18] The Lord will rescue me from every evil deed and bring me safely into his heavenly kingdom. To him be the glory forever and ever. Amen.

### Final Greetings

[19] Greet Prisca and Aquila, and the household of Onesiphorus. [20] Erastus remained at Corinth, and I left Trophimus, who was ill, at Miletus. [21] Do your best to come before winter. Eubulus sends greetings to you, as do Pudens and Linus and Claudia and all the brothers.

[22] The Lord be with your spirit. Grace be with you.

# TITUS

### Greeting

1 Paul, a servant of God and an apostle of Jesus Christ, for the sake of the faith of God's elect and their knowledge of the truth, which accords with godliness, ² in hope of eternal life, which God, who never lies, promised before the ages began ³ and at the proper time manifested in his word through the preaching with which I have been entrusted by the command of God our Savior;

⁴ To Titus, my true child in a common faith:

Grace and peace from God the Father and Christ Jesus our Savior.

### Qualifications for Elders

⁵ This is why I left you in Crete, so that you might put what remained into order, and appoint elders in every town as I directed you— ⁶ if anyone is above reproach, the husband of one wife, and his children are believers and not open to the charge of debauchery or insubordination. ⁷ For an overseer, as God's steward, must be above reproach. He must not be arrogant or quick-tempered or a drunkard or violent or greedy for gain, ⁸ but hospitable, a lover of good, self-controlled, upright, holy, and disciplined. ⁹ He must hold firm to the trustworthy word as taught, so that he may be able to give

instruction in sound doctrine and also to rebuke those who contradict it.

[10] For there are many who are insubordinate, empty talkers and deceivers, especially those of the circumcision party. [11] They must be silenced, since they are upsetting whole families by teaching for shameful gain what they ought not to teach. [12] One of the Cretans, a prophet of their own, said, "Cretans are always liars, evil beasts, lazy gluttons." [13] This testimony is true. Therefore rebuke them sharply, that they may be sound in the faith, [14] not devoting themselves to Jewish myths and the commands of people who turn away from the truth. [15] To the pure, all things are pure, but to the defiled and unbelieving, nothing is pure; but both their minds and their consciences are defiled. [16] They profess to know God, but they deny him by their works. They are detestable, disobedient, unfit for any good work.

### Teach Sound Doctrine

2 But as for you, teach what accords with sound doctrine. [2] Older men are to be sober-minded, dignified, self-controlled, sound in faith, in love, and in steadfastness. [3] Older women likewise are to be reverent in behavior, not slanderers or slaves to much wine. They are to teach what is good, [4] and so train the young women to love their husbands and children, [5] to be self-controlled, pure, working at home, kind, and submissive to their own husbands, that the word of God may not be reviled. [6] Likewise, urge the younger men to be self-controlled. [7] Show yourself in all respects to be a model of good works, and in your teaching show integrity, dignity, [8] and sound speech that cannot be condemned, so that an opponent may be put to shame, having nothing evil to say about us. [9] Bondservants

are to be submissive to their own masters in everything; they are to be well-pleasing, not argumentative, [10] not pilfering, but showing all good faith, so that in everything they may adorn the doctrine of God our Savior.

[11] For the grace of God has appeared, bringing salvation for all people, [12] training us to renounce ungodliness and worldly passions, and to live self-controlled, upright, and godly lives in the present age, [13] waiting for our blessed hope, the appearing of the glory of our great God and Savior Jesus Christ, [14] who gave himself for us to redeem us from all lawlessness and to purify for himself a people for his own possession who are zealous for good works.

[15] Declare these things; exhort and rebuke with all authority. Let no one disregard you.

*Be Ready for Every Good Work*

3 Remind them to be submissive to rulers and authorities, to be obedient, to be ready for every good work, [2] to speak evil of no one, to avoid quarreling, to be gentle, and to show perfect courtesy toward all people. [3] For we ourselves were once foolish, disobedient, led astray, slaves to various passions and pleasures, passing our days in malice and envy, hated by others and hating one another. [4] But when the goodness and loving kindness of God our Savior appeared, [5] he saved us, not because of works done by us in righteousness, but according to his own mercy, by the washing of regeneration and renewal of the Holy Spirit, [6] whom he poured out on us richly through Jesus Christ our Savior, [7] so that being justified by his grace we might become heirs according to the hope of eternal life. [8] The saying is trustworthy, and I want you to insist on these things, so that those

who have believed in God may be careful to devote themselves to good works. These things are excellent and profitable for people. ⁹ But avoid foolish controversies, genealogies, dissensions, and quarrels about the law, for they are unprofitable and worthless. ¹⁰ As for a person who stirs up division, after warning him once and then twice, have nothing more to do with him, ¹¹ knowing that such a person is warped and sinful; he is self-condemned.

### Final Instructions and Greetings

¹² When I send Artemas or Tychicus to you, do your best to come to me at Nicopolis, for I have decided to spend the winter there. ¹³ Do your best to speed Zenas the lawyer and Apollos on their way; see that they lack nothing. ¹⁴ And let our people learn to devote themselves to good works, so as to help cases of urgent need, and not be unfruitful.

¹⁵ All who are with me send greetings to you. Greet those who love us in the faith.

Grace be with you all.